THE WHOLE ARMOR OF GOD

Published

&

Printed

By

EDMAZ Sole Publisher

ISBN 978-0-7974-8366-8

All Biblical Quotations Are From THE NEW KING JAMES VERSION.

DEDICATION

With all my heart, all my soul and my entire mind, I completely dedicate this book to all the believers of Jesus Christ who seek physical and spiritual deliverance, and to those that desire to be mighty warriors in the Kingdom of God. To such, may the grace of the true and living God – The God of Abraham, Isaac and Jacob – come in abundance. Amen.

ACKNOWLEDGEMENTS

With much respect and honor, I acknowledge the Servant and Apostle of God Dr. E. H. Guti for inspiring me to write this book. Secondly, I express my gratitude to my fellow relatives in Christ with whom I ministered at ZAOGA Bindura Cathedral. Those were Happy Mhlanga, Evangelist Roncemore Mhlanga, Elder Stanley Mapurazi, Joseph Mugambo, Elder Baba and Eldress Amai Chabayanzara, Tafadzwa Kabadzimu, Br. Ben Bunhure, Leonard Mandima and many others. They supported me in many ways.

Out of the centre of blessings, I cannot leave Aisha Chigodo and Happy Mhlanga. God mightily used them to provide me with all the food I ate during my prayers. Blessings from above should follow them in Jesus Christ's name. Amen!

Separately, I thank God for Prophet John Moyounotsva and Pastor Anna Moyounotsva who molded me to be what I am in Christianity. Those were the servants of God with whom He allowed me to stay during His pruning me.

Glory, be unto the Lord God.

INTRODUCTION

I wrote this book in 2009 and 2010 when I was at ZAOGA Cathedral Prayer Mountain in Bindura. For those that may need to know more about this place, it is found in Zimbabwe, a country that is located in the continent of Africa.

This book provides with teachings that are chiefly set to educate people about putting on the whole armor of God so that they may be able to stand against the wiles of the devil.

God revealed it that it is wise and necessary to let people comprehend this armor; for ignorance to it has vaguely risen to be a fundamental problem that vastly hinders people from achieving complete and permanent deliverance to their lives. In this way, the answer to the problem is to let people know so that they will not perish, for the Bible says in Hosea 4 vs. 6: *'My people are destroyed for lack of knowledge.'*

Our God allowed me to write about each and every weapon of His armor mentioned by Paul in the book of Ephesians. He also permitted me to touch the devils just to rip off their faces. The good news is: God's desire is to bring physical and spiritual deliverance to any believing reader of this book. In Jesus Christ's name, I shout, "Amen!"

These teachings are mainly based on Ephesians 6 vs. 10 – 19. At the end, I teach and urge the reader to persevere in Christ. Amen.

NOTE: I assure you in the name of Jesus Christ that deliverance will take place as you will be reading this book with faith.

MAY GOD BLESS YOU, AMEN!

CONTENTS

1. Opening Prayer...7
2. The Ephesians...8
3. Paul's love for the Ephesians................................9
4. Be strong in the Lord...13
5. The whole armor of God...15
6. We do not wrestle against flesh and blood..........16
7. Be able to withstand in the evil day....................23
8. Gird your waist with truth.................................24
9. Put on the breastplate of righteousness..............25
10. The preparation of the gospel of peace.................26
11. The shield of faith...26
12. The helmet of salvation...28
13. The sword of the spirit..32
14. Prayer and supplication.......................................33
15. Perseverance and supplication............................37
16. Closing Prayer...43

1. OPENING PRAYER

Precious God who dwells in Heaven between the
cherubim,

Great and awesome is your name, Jehovah; the
Almighty Warrior; the Lion of the Tribe of Judah.

Father, the Almighty Warrior, I pray that you fight for
me and deliver me from the hands of the devil as I
peruse this book.

I pray for my deliverance and for my knowledge from
your teachings.

O my God, open my mind that I understand your
Word, and guide me that I will not go astray.

In the name of Jesus Christ, I say, "Amen."

2. THE EPHESIANS

The plural noun, **Ephesians**, refers to the people who lived in Ephesus, an ancient Greek city. Today, it is found in the Western Turkey.

Ephesus found grace from God through Apostle Paul who preached to it about Jesus Christ. Some of the people in it repented but others did not.

In this way, it became a spiritual challenge to the saints who had received Christ as they mingled with the pagans that had not received Him at all. Their Christianity was gradually being eaten away by pagandom until Paul wrote an epistle to them. He did so to channel them into the true Way of God.

Paul was an apostle to the Gentiles. He was called by God through a mighty way *(Acts 9 vs. 3-20)*. Before he received Jesus Christ as his personal Savior, he was a murderer, and his name was Saul. He used to kill the Christians.

God is great and awesome indeed! This same God is still able to change our wicked backgrounds. He can make us new people today. Amen!

3. PAUL'S LOVE FOR THE EPHESIANS

In general, laws are introduced after crimes have been committed. In the same way, corrections come after mistakes have occurred, and so, does counseling after trouble has taken place.

Paul, an apostle of Jesus Christ by the will of God *(Ephesians 1 vs. 1)*, wrote to the saints who were in Ephesus. He showed his love by correcting and teaching them the way to live well among others after he had noticed an unusual conduct among them.

Like I said, corrections come after mistakes have occurred. After noting that the saints in Ephesus were walking as pagans, Paul wrote to them: *"....you should no longer walk as the rest of the Gentiles walk...."* *Ephesians 4 vs. 17*

The Gentiles that Paul warned not to be imitated were walking in bad, displeasing ways. There were among them fornication, uncleanness, covetousness, filthiness, idolatry, foolish talking, and so on. Hence, Paul warned the saints not to let such behavior even be named among them as is fitting for saints *(Ephesians 5 vs. 3)*.

Paul advised them to see then that they walked circumspectly, not as fools but as wise, redeeming the time, because the days are evil (Ephesians 5 vs. 15-16). He also taught them to submit to one another (Eph. 5 vs. 21). Wives were advised to submit to their husbands (Eph. 5 vs. 22), and children to obey their parents (Eph. 6 vs. 1). Fathers were told not to provoke their children to wrath (Eph. 6 vs. 4). Servants were advised to obey their masters according to the flesh (Eph. 6 vs. 5), and masters to do the same to their servants knowing that their own Master also is in Heaven (Eph. 6 vs. 9).

Dear fellow believers, it is clear that there were conflicts between wives and husbands; parents and children and masters and servants. If it was not like that, Paul would not waste his strength and time on them because there is no a normal person who corrects the correct. There were really conflicts among the saints in Ephesus.

Marriage Conflicts

The marriage conflict that existed between a husband and a wife in Ephesus may be the same with the one in which you and your partner are. There is no longer submission in your marriage. You no longer accept advice from each other. You usually blame each other for any silly mistake. No one likes to be under control of the other.

Dear believer, you are in the bondage of the evil spirits that work in the Marriage Spoiling Department. Open your mind. Do not waste your time fighting against your spouse. We do not fight against flesh and blood, but against spirits.

You do not need a man or a woman of God to lay hands on you in order that you get delivered from this. You simply need to change your attitude towards your spouse. Good attitude needs exercise and prayer.

Family Conflicts

The family conflict that was between the fathers and their children in Ephesus may be the same with the one in your family. There is no longer love or trust between a parent and a child. There is suspicion and hatred. The father thinks the child is not his and that he might have been deceived by his wife. The child also hates his or her father because he discriminates him or her from the family.

There may be a lot of incidents other than this in your family that are causing tensions right now. All this is the work of the evil spirits in the Family Spoiling Department. Wake up and stop fighting against one another. You need prayers for your family and bring it up in a godly manner.

Work Conflicts

Some work conflicts that occurred between a servant and his master in Ephesus may be the same with the ones that are present at your workplace today. Your master suspects that you always steal from his or her coffers. Thus, he or she does not give you a satisfactory pay. Because of this, you hate him or her and always complain.

In this case, both of you, the servant and the master, are victims of the evil spirits. You need to trust each other. Both of you must be reliable.

In my life, I came to realize that everything that happens on earth happens under the influence of a spirit – it may be a spirit from God, or from the devil. Spirits influence people to carry out some actions that may be good or bad. Therefore, it is wiser to deal with the influencing spirits than the influenced person. Fighting against the influenced person shows immaturity in your spirit. Instead of going against the influenced which is flesh and blood, go against the influencer which is the spirit.

Paul noticed the problem among the Ephesians and identified its causer, the devil whom the Ephesians had not acknowledged. The apostle's love was for them to live in peace without conflicts and imitation of ungodly custom from the rest of the Gentiles (Eph. 4 vs. 17). He urged them to be strong in the Lord and in the power of His might (Eph. 6 vs. 10).

The spirits that badly influenced the life of the Ephesians a very, very long time ago are the ones that are ill-treating this generation of today. People are going against one another in families, churches, at work and in marriages. Almost in the whole world, people have turned against one another. They are confused and tossed to and fro by these evil spirits.

But now, Paul says, *"Finally, my brethren, be strong in the Lord and in the power of His might." Eph. 6 vs. 10*

4. BE STRONG IN THE LORD

Finally, my brethren, be strong in the Lord and in the power of His might (Eph. 6 vs. 10).

In this verse, Paul says, *"Finally..."* which means *"At the end..."* *"...be strong..."* He knew that many people are defeated at the end as they try to taste rest. I have also witnessed, with my naked eyes, many competitors who were unexpectedly defeated in the final minutes. In general, all competitions that are governed with time limit become tougher as they draw near to finishing points.

Likewise, the spiritual warfare between the devil and us increases in weight as we draw near the end of the world. Persecutions and tribulations grow bigger in a fierce way. This forces some believers to quit Jesus Christ. Therefore, Paul – because of all these troubles – urges us to be strong in the Lord and in the power of His might. Amen.

To be strong in the Lord is to stand immovable with all trust in Jesus Christ gripping the power of His authority as the 'son' in His Kingdom. You ought to depend on the power of God's might, not on that one of yours. Your own might is nothing to the spiritual warfare.

The Bible – Zechariah 4 vs. 6 – says, "'Not by might nor by power, but by My Spirit,' says the Lord of hosts."

It is the Spirit of God that torments the spirits of the devil, not our own might or power.

What is bound by the spirit is set free by the other spirit, not by the flesh. So, it is the Spirit of God that is able to set free those that are in the ties of the evil spirits. This is the reason Jesus Christ read from the book of Isaiah: "The Spirit of the Lord is upon me, *because He has anointed me...to preach deliverance to the captives...to set at liberty those who are oppressed..." Luke 4 vs. 18.*

If the Spirit of God was not upon Jesus Christ, he would not set at liberty those who were oppressed or those who were in captivity. It is only the Spirit of God that brings deliverance to those that are in bondage of evil spirits.

Our own power is nothing. Hence, let us all depend on the Spirit of God for power so that we conquer the devil.

5. THE WHOLE ARMOR OF GOD

Put on the whole armor of God, that you may be able to stand against the wiles of the devil. Eph. 6 vs. 11

Having urged the Ephesians to be strong in the Lord, Paul told them to put on the whole armor of God that they might be able to stand against the wiles of the devil. It is not good just to stand in the Lord without wearing His armor. If you just stand without the whole armor of God, you will not be able to stand against the wiles of the devil. This is why many Christians are the victims of the devil instead of being the victors.

The reason is just that many people join churches to be refuges, not to be soldiers, and they do not mind to carry even a single weapon. Such believers are miserable victims of the devil.

To those that come to the Lord to be victorious soldiers, the apostle gives instruction to put on the whole armor of God. This armor must be put on in whole. It will not do the best for a person who puts it on, but not in complete attire.

This armor is of God, not of man. The armor of man has no deal with this type of warfare. The weapons of this warfare are not carnal, but mighty in God for pulling down strongholds *(2 Corinthians 10 vs. 4)*.

These weapons – to testify the truth – cause every demonic spirit to shake or tremble with great fear. This is why they are said to be mighty for pulling down strongholds. So, let us all put on the whole armor of God and stand firm in the Lord to fight our enemies.

6. WE DO NOT WRESTLE AGAINST FLESH AND BLOOD

For we do not wrestle against flesh and blood, but against principalities, against powers, against the rulers of the darkness of this age, against spiritual hosts of wickedness in the heavenly places. Eph. 6 vs. 12

When we put on the whole armor of God, we stand firm in the Lord and in the power of His might to fight our enemies. And our enemies are not our neighbors or those who bewitch or persecute us. We do not have to fight these relatives of ours. Instead, we should pray for them because they are also the victims of the evil spirits as they are.

Fighting against them is to lack wisdom in spirit. We have to fight the devil who tied them to loosen his hold and go. As it is in the case of an eagle and a chick, when the eagle snatches the chick away from the ground, the owner of the chick cannot seize a catapult to hit the chick, but he seizes it to hit the eagle instead. When the eagle is hit, it releases the chick. So, when these evil spirits are hit, they loosen their grip and release the victim. Amen.

We do not fight against the man, but against all the demonic angels, forces and spirits that seek to deceive and torment them.

Apostle Paul shows it clearly that we do not wrestle against flesh and blood, but against principalities, against powers, against the rulers of the darkness of this age and against spiritual hosts of wickedness in the heavenly places. Hallelujah! These are the right enemies we are putting on the whole armor of God for, not man.

Principalities

Eph. 6 vs. 12...*against principalities*... These are demonic spirits that have been operating from ancient times. Theirs is to trace each and every family blood introducing and passing on negative principles of life from one or more members of the family to the other. For instance, in a certain family, the principle of life applied to it by these principalities from ancient times may work mathematically in this way: $1 = 0$; this means one is equal to zero. On actual ground, it means each member in the family, especially the victim of these spirits, is equal to nobody. Such member is the one that others call or say: *"Hapana zvemunhu"* or "He/she is nothing."

Dear believer, do not entertain a person who says to you: "You are nothing in life" or "You are useless in life."

These evil spirits may find support from such negative words upon you, and as a result, they invade you.

Powers

Eph. 6 vs. 12...*against powers*... These are demonic spirits with delegated power to operate everywhere exerting pressure, power or forces upon situations or anything else to be too complicated. The power that they apply is negative to or against the power of God.

The rulers of the darkness of this age

Eph. 6 vs. 12...*against the rulers of the darkness of this age*... They are demonic spirits that establish rules to run the system of this world. They are in charge of the darkness of this age. They are the ones that order worldly activities to be performed in churches. They torment and spoil people in different ages. The youth are tormented in a way that they become weird and misbehave before elderly people or their parents.

These spirits win the youth's mind to say: "This is the modern world; things have changed. We do as we are pleased, not as our parents are."

What this generation does not know is: it does not do as it is pleased, but as the devil is pleased. It is unaware of the fact that it is under the ruling of these spirits.

Spiritual hosts of wickedness

Eph. 6 vs. 12...*against spiritual hosts of wickedness*... These demonic spirits are fully packed with all wickedness or iniquity. Their name speaks on its own that they are hosts of wickedness. They harbor or accommodate wickedness. Their duty is to inflict people with evil, to corrode their hearts with bitterness and cause damages to the souls. They do even more than this.

A funny thing with all the spirits that Apostle Paul mentioned is that they work hand in hand to achieve their goals. Their unity is so challenging that I wonder why Christians are not as united as they are. You know what? Christians seem to be defeated simply because they lack unity and commitment.

Dear believer, let us be united because there is power in unity, and that power is a threat to the devil. Our unity baffles the devil and forces the unity in his kingdom to disintegrate. If we are not united, the unity of the demons is consolidated.

Demons also work in departments. There are several departments of them. One man of God whose name is Dag Heward-Mills listed down some of the teams of these demons in his book titled: DEMONS AND HOW TO DEAL WITH THEM. I learnt much from this book.

There are demons that work in the Marriage Spoiling team. These are always busy trying to part each and every couple. They bring great confusion in marriages either through the wives or through the husbands, or through any other person from outside. Sometimes, they work in connection with the spirits in the Sex team which put themselves in position to influence the partners to commit adultery. All they need is to destroy marriages.

The Sex team is a group in which there are demons of adultery and fornication. The demons of adultery influence one not to be satisfied with one's partner and forces one to search for an outdoor sex-partner.

The spirits of fornication – unlike the spirits of adultery – deal with unmarried people. They influence them to have unauthorized sex with each other. These spirits may work in collaboration with the spirits from the Future Spoiling team which works to spoil young people's future. Unfortunately, some young people had their future spoiled when they were still at school. Others had it spoiled soon after school, and so on. May our Lord God have mercy on such people, in Jesus name. Amen and amen.

The devil is a liar. He tried to destroy the whole of you. Today, Jesus Christ is knocking at the door of your heart with a new life for you. He needs to transform you into a new you. May you open the door for Him for your renovations? Amen.

There is also the other team: the Church Spoiling team. This team works to destroy unity in churches. It causes Christians to find faults with one another, to practise gossip against one another and to hate one another. That is why you see instability in churches continues with great confusion. It is all because of these spirits. We need to disagree with them in order to conquer them. We need to do away with all gossip, all hatred and all fault-finding, and begin to practise righteousness and establish unity in love. Once we do so, we cast the devil away. Hallelujah.

There are other teams or departments of demons which I have not mentioned.

Among the demons that Apostle Paul mentioned, there are some that are as territorial as enzymes. Enzymes have limited areas where they are active. For example, an amylase enzyme is active in the mouth, but not in the stomach. If the amylase enzyme proceeds to the stomach, it will die. The same applies to the territorial demons, they are active in one territory, but not in another. In Mark 5 vs. 10, such demons feared to be cast out of the country by Jesus Christ. They really knew that they were only active and powerful in that country, but not in another.

Mark 5 vs. 10 reads: *And he begged Him earnestly that He would not send them out of the country.*

Some areas have territorial demons of poverty. I noticed a number of well people who shifted to certain places where there were territorial demons of poverty. When they reached those places, they began to sell all their possessions and were left destitute.

Another occasion is the story Dinah (Genesis 34 vs. 1-2). She was attacked by territorial demons of fornication in the land of Canaan.

Dear believer, you have to know that every country or area has got demons of its own. Therefore, I urge you to make a fervent prayer whenever you reach any country or area. Hallelujah.

7. BE ABLE TO WITHSTAND IN THE EVIL DAY

Therefore take up the whole armor of God, that you may be able to withstand in the evil day, and having done all, to stand. Eph. 6 vs. 13

It is transparent in this verse that you may not be able to withstand in the evil day without taking up the whole armor of God. A soldier who confronts his enemy will not stand the war if he does so without adequate weapons.

Many Christians have been severely victimized by the devil because they lack spiritual weapons. They are weak soldiers who dread to burden themselves with weapons. Some, however, are not weak, but it is only that they lack knowledge about these spiritual weapons. The Bible says in Hosea 4 vs. 6: *'My people are destroyed for lack of knowledge.'*

8. GIRD YOUR WAIST WITH TRUTH

...having girded your waist with truth...Eph. 6 vs. 14

Apostle Paul did not leave us with questions about spiritual weapons. After telling the Ephesians to put on the whole armor of God, he went on to tell them what those weapons in the armor of God were, and how they were to be put on. The first weapon that Apostle Paul spoke of was the belt of truth. You know what? I watched some ancient pictures of Roman soldiers who existed in the times of Apostle Paul. They were completely armored. Their waists were girded with what I may simply call belts, but they were not ordinary belts; they were girds. Those girds provided with protection to the soldier's waist. These are the ones Paul is taking for truth in the Bible.

Thus, a Christian who lacks the truth lacks this belt, and he or she finds it hard to withstand in the evil day. A Christian should always exercise to tell the truth. This truth is the belt of our spiritual warfare. Hallelujah.

9. PUT ON THE BREASTPLATE OF RIGHTEOUSNESS

...having put on the breastplate of righteousness...Eph. 6 vs. 14

The second weapon that Apostle Paul mentioned was the breastplate. This weapon serves to protect the soldier's chest. Without it, the chest is ruined. If the chest is ruined, the heart of the soldier is also ruined. Do you get the sense of it? This breastplate is the breastplate of righteousness, and this means: if the breastplate is not there, righteousness is not there. If righteousness is not there, the heart – a spiritual heart – is ruined by evil spirits, and the person may be possessed of them.

Do not take this weapon for granted. A person should always exercise righteousness, and he who practices it is born of God (John 2 vs. 29). So, let us all exercise this righteousness of God. It is one of our spiritual weapons to fight the devil with. Hallelujah.

10. THE PREPARATION OF THE GOSPEL OF PEACE

*...having shod your feet with the preparation of the gospel of peace...*Eph. 6 vs. 15

The preparation of the gospel of peace is the third weapon that Apostle Paul talked of as army shoes. The army-shoes protect a soldier as he steps on sharp, harmful obstacles. The shoes also hurt the enemy when he is kicked by the soldier. So, the preparation of the gospel of peace is a dangerous weapon to our enemy, the devil.

Every believer has to prepare the gospel of peace. The gospel of peace is the gospel of Jesus Christ. A person who lacks it lacks the combat shoes. Hence, he gets pierced and hurt easily by sharp obstacles in his way. Many believers collapse because they lack the gospel of peace. Hallelujah.

11. THE SHIELD OF FAITH

...above all, taking the shield of faith with which you will be able to quench all the fiery darts of the wicked one. Eph. 6 vs. 16

A shield is anything that is used to stop harmful weapons of the enemy from reaching the one handling it. The Roman soldiers in the times of Apostle Paul used shields to prevent spears, arrows or any other harmful object from reaching them.

These shields are large, strong and portable. They may be of different sizes and shapes but they serve the same purpose. I apologize that I cannot give you further descriptions of them.

Apostle Paul discovered then that the shield is like faith in such a way that it quenches spears, swords or arrows from the enemy. Faith quenches the fiery darts of the wicked one. Without faith, a believer cannot stand in the battle with the devil. It is also impossible to please God without faith (Hebrews 11 vs. 6).

The shield which is the fourth weapon spoken of by Paul is needed by every believer to quench the fiery darts of the devil. The fiery darts of the devil are those things that the devil throws to intimidate us. These things appear real but they are not. They have never been and will never be real. If you have no faith, they bring fear to you.

One of the fiery darts is the false death-predicting dream. Satan may show you a tragedy-nightmare in which you are a main victim who soon ends in death. If you have no faith, this dream will cause you great fear. It may make you have no hope for life and cause you to squander all your property thinking that you may die any time.

If you have faith, you acknowledge your position in Jesus Christ and know that the Almighty Lord God cannot let such an evil thing happen to your life because He has got great plans with you which need to be accomplished on earth. There is no weapon formed against the child of God that shall prosper. Thus says the Word of God in Isaiah 54 vs. 17.

Dear friend, do not dread the fiery darts of the devil. Just hold the shield of faith and use it to quench them. Hallelujah.

12. THE HELMET OF SALVATION

*And take the helmet of salvation...*Eph. 6 vs. 17

The fifth weapon is the helmet of salvation. Generally, a helmet, as we know it, is put on to protect the head of the person wearing it. A soldier who goes to war without this helmet is likely to have his head throbbed by his enemy.

Every believer must wear this helmet of salvation to cover the brain in his or her head so that the deceiver fails to attack and put it under his control. Hallelujah.

Salvation has to be sought. If you do not seek it, you will not find it.

Let us look at Zacchaeus who happened to have salvation in his house:

Luke, chapter 19, verses:

2 Now behold, there was a man named Zacchaeus who was a chief tax collector, and he was rich.

3 And he sought to see who Jesus was, but could not because of the crowd, for he was of short stature.

4 So he ran ahead and climbed up a sycamore tree to see Him, for He was going to pass that way.

5 And when Jesus came to the place, He looked up and saw him, and said to him, "Zacchaeus, make haste and come down, for today I must stay at your house."

6 So he made haste and came down, and received Him joyfully.

7 But they saw it, they all murmured, saying, "He has gone to be a guest with a man who is a sinner."

8 Then Zacchaeus stood and said to the Lord, "Look, Lord, I give half of my goods to the poor; and if I have taken anything from anyone by false accusation, I restore fourfold."

9 And Jesus said to him, "Today salvation has come to this house, because he is also a son of Abraham;

10 "For the Son of Man has come to seek and to save that which was lost."

Some people say salvation is a process. I agree with these people. If we look at Zacchaeus, we see that it was a process for him to have salvation announced in his house, (Luke 19 vs. 9). You know what? – If you saw Zacchaeus in the first place following Jesus Christ like others, you would think that he also knew Jesus, and that salvation was already in his house, but it was not like that. He had to seek the face of Jesus first for salvation to be proclaimed in his house.

Zacchaeus sought to see who Jesus was, but could not because of the crowd, for he was of short stature, (Luke 19 vs. 3). The crowd was a serious obstacle to him. It could not give him chance to see the Lord and have his salvation.

If you look at it today, it is the crowd that avoids you to see Jesus Christ and to have your salvation. It always discourages you in whatever you try to do in order to mature in Christ and achieve your salvation.

I like what Zacchaeus did, he quickly noticed that the whole trouble was coming from the crowd. Therefore, he ran ahead of it and climbed up a sycamore tree (Luke 19 vs. 4) to be where no other man was. In the same way, you have to keep yourself from discouraging people if you want to enjoy Jesus Christ.

When Jesus saw that Zacchaeus had sought Him, He called him saying, *"Zacchaeus, make haste and come down, for today I must stay at your house."* Luke 19 vs. 5.

The Lord calls to stay with you when He sees that your struggle is to know Him. People may all complain why the Lord has called you, but that will not change God's favor on you. Dear friends, the Lord who blesses will lift you up and set a table for you before your enemies. Just seek Him, He will see you. It is just the matter of seeking and finding Jesus Christ in order that you find salvation, the helmet of war.

When Jesus was in the house of Zacchaeus, He pronounced that salvation had come in that house. He said that soon after Zacchaeus had blurted out that he gave half of his goods to the poor; and that if he had taken anything from anyone by false accusation, he restored fourfold (Luke 19 vs. 8). He regretted it because Jesus Christ had come into his house with salvation.

If you are a Christian who does not regret stinginess and cheating as Zacchaeus did, it means Jesus Christ has not yet pronounced salvation in your house (heart) although you are His follower. It means you are an ordinary follower like what Zacchaeus was before he was called.

Let us all seek salvation by quitting evil. Salvation is the helmet of war. Hallelujah.

13. THE SWORD OF THE SPIRIT

...and the sword of the Spirit, which is the word of God...Eph. 6 vs. 17

The sixth weapon is the sword of the Spirit which is the Word of God. The Word of God – though it is likened to a real sword – is living and powerful. It is sharper than any two-edged sword piercing even to the division of the soul and the spirit, and of joints and marrow, and is a discerner of the thoughts and intents of the heart (Hebrews 4 vs. 12).

This is very, very powerful indeed. To testify the truth, the Word of God is the only 'sword' that strikes evil spirits away from you. All demons – I mean all of them in all their classes – dread the Word of God. They quiver when they hear of it. When you increase in the Word of God, demons decrease in power, but when you decrease, they increase.

A person who knows very little of the Word of God owns a blunt sword, and with it, he struggles to defeat his enemy. You need to sharpen your sword by perusing the Bible and meditating upon its scriptures. Some people are severely victimized by the evil spirits because they reject the use of the sword, the Word of God.

In the times of Apostle Paul, the Roman soldiers used the swords to strike down their enemies. In this manner, we, as Christians, use the Word of God to strike down the devil, our enemy. Without the Word of God, we cannot conquer him. Hallelujah.

14. PRAYER AND SUPPLICATION

*...praying always with all prayer and supplication in the Spirit...*Eph. 6 vs. 18

Apostle Paul urged the Ephesians to pray always with all prayer and supplication in the Spirit. He urged them to do so because the enemy makes confrontation day and night without rest.

Satan with his kingdom is the one against whom we make all prayers and supplication. Prayers should be made in Spirit because the warfare is spiritual, and must be fervent. Many people testify that fervent prayers produce results, and this is true.

I know, you may be eager to know what this fervent prayer is. You need to make it. Let me tell you something about it: a fervent prayer is a powerful prayer that you make with all your heart, all your soul and your entire mind in the Spirit of the Lord. This prayer exalts the name of the Lord. It casts down all demonic forces and pulls down strongholds. It breaks every bound of the devil. Every demon dreads such a prayer.

The devil does not fear any person who goes without prayers. You must know this.

Paul said, *"...and supplication..."* Supplication and prayer are one – supplication is in prayer; and prayer is in supplication. In supplication, you make intercession. This is far better than making a selfish prayer. God is not interested in a prayer that is selfish. Learn to intercede for everyone: your family members, friends, church-leaders, every authority and those who persecute you.

Do not marvel that I have said intercede for those who persecute you. In Luke 6 vs. 27-28, Jesus Christ spoke thus: *"...love your enemies, do good to those who hate you, bless those who curse you, and pray for those who spitefully use you."*

A prayer – as I learnt from other teachers – is made out of an abbreviation, **ACTS**. This abbreviation stands for **A**doration, **C**onfession, **T**hanksgiving and **S**upplication.

Adoration

This is whereby you praise and worship God showing Him your love. In this way, you exalt His name either by singing or by speaking of His excellence. By so doing, you create the atmosphere of His manifested presence. The Lord dwells in the praises of His saints. When you praise Him, God appears. So, learn to start your prayer with a warm presentation of praises better than that of complaints to Him. Remember Paul and Silas in ACTS 16 vs. 25-26. When they were in prison, instead of complaining, they praised God, and He appeared to them. Hallelujah.

Confession

Now, confession follows soon after you have created the atmosphere of God's manifested presence. Confession is disclosing all your sins to Jesus Christ even though He knows them all. Without confession, you will not be healed or answered your prayer. James 5 vs. 16.

Thanksgiving

This is whereby you give thanks to God for that entire He did, or has done, or is doing for you. You may also thank Him for the things that He is doing for other people. You thank Him for forgiving you your sins. Though you do not hear God saying audibly that He has forgiven you soon after confession, you just know by faith that if you confess your sins, He is faithful and just to forgive you your sins and to cleanse you from all unrighteousness (1 John 1 vs. 9). Amen.

Supplication

Supplication is whereby you pray and intercede for your needs and those of others. Hallelujah.

All is done in the Spirit just as Apostle Paul said: "...*all prayer and supplication in the Spirit*..." Eph. 6 vs. 18

15. PERSEVERANCE AND SUPPLICATION

...being watchful to this end with all perseverance and supplication for all saints...Eph. 6 vs. 18

Paul, an apostle of Jesus Christ by the will of God, warned the saints about the end and urged them to persevere with supplication. To persevere is to persist with patience throughout difficulties. The other word that may be used in place of it is 'endure'.

The saints in Ephesus were facing challenges; that is why Apostle Paul urged them to persevere: "...*with...perseverance*..."

Challenges are always available with us on this earth. It is so normal that we face them. There are outdoor and indoor challenges. The outdoor challenges are those that are brought to us by the outsiders. The indoor ones are those that come with the people we always associate with.

Challenges make us mature in spirit. They make us change for better. The Servant and Apostle of God E. H. Guti wrote a book titled: HUMAN BEINGS CAN NOT

CHANGE WITHOUT PRESSURE. This is true. Human beings need pressure to change for better. This pressure is what we call challenge.

Pressure is always there to make you change for better, but if you resist it, it kills you.

Joseph did not just become a man of God from nowhere. He had to go through difficulties. He was once cast into a pit by his own brothers (Genesis 37 vs. 24). Later on, he was sold from the pit to be a slave (Genesis 37 vs. 28). In Egypt, he was accused of attempted rape (Genesis 39 vs. 14-18), and he was put in prison for that.

Joseph suffered indoor challenges from his own brothers, and from Potiphar's wife.

In churches, there are some indoor challenges that we face from our own fellow church-members. These challenges are tougher and more painful than those that we face from the 'world'.

Sometimes, you may see a church that sought you through preaching going against you. This is usual. It also happened to Elisha. Elisha was sought by Elijah (1 Kings 19 vs. 19-21), but after that, came a certain occasion when he was being sent away by the same man who had called him (2 Kings 2 vs. 1-6). If Elisha was as impatient as many of us are today, he would not persist in following Elijah, and would not get a double portion of Elijah's spirit (2 Kings 2 vs. 9-13). Amen.

Dear believer, when you fall into various trials, count it all joy (James 1 vs. 2). The Lord does not leave you alone when you are in trouble. Shadrack, Abed-Nego and Meshack were not left alone in the pit of fire (Daniel 3 vs. 24-25). This is the way that God uses to prepare His mighty warriors. Hallelujah.

In the case of David, he was being hunted for his dear life by Saul (1 Samuel 19 vs. 9-10), the very person who had called him to serve in his house (1 Samuel 17 vs. 21-22). So, do not worry about those people in church who were showing their love to you in the first days, but nowadays, they are not. People are people.

You must know that the more the presence of God intensifies, the more the troubles from the devil come. The devil is like a dog. When it barks in the night, it barks at moving things, not at stationary ones.

The devil mainly troubles those with whom God has greater plans. When you are already cool in the Kingdom of God, he (the devil) has no big deal with you. Remember King Pharaoh and his men, they planned to kill every Hebrew boy to be born, but save every girl. Likewise, the devil and his followers seek to murder those people who are hot in the things of God, but not those that are cool.

If you are a Christian who goes smoothly all the way without any temptation, trial or test, you need to check your position. You might have already stopped burning in spirit. It is usual to face challenges as a Christian, and unusual not to face them. Jesus Christ faced them too. So, why can't you?

Dear Christians, challenges are not permitted by God to weaken us, but to strengthen us. Hallelujah. So, let us all persevere in order that we achieve our goals.

Samson was born a strong man, but he needed some provocation from his enemies (the Philistines) in order for him to use his power. One day, he caught three hundred foxes. He tied their tails to make a total number of one hundred and fifty pairs, and then attached torches to their tails. The foxes ran across the fields of the Philistines and burnt them to ashes (Judges 15 vs. 4-5). Samson did so because he had faced a challenge from his Philistine father in-law who had given his (Samson's) wife to his (Samson's) best man at the wedding (Judges 14 vs. 20).

~ 40 ~

Your pace in life is determined by the challenges you face. Challenges are like steps on a ladder; they lead us up. If they are not available, we will not go up.

May the Lord God strengthen us when we face them. Hallelujah. We need endurance. We need to go forward in faith. Dear Christians, there are rewards ahead that the Lord set for those that persevere with supplication. The Lord will give power over nations to him who overcomes, and keeps His work to the end (Revelation 2 vs. 26).

In Eph. 6 vs. 18, Paul said, "...*being watchful to this end...*" He was right to warn us like that. We have to be watchful to this end as we persevere so that we do not do it for nothing. Many people have been deceived by the devil, and have unknowingly persevered in the things that are not of God.

Dear friend, be watchful to this end. False prophets have spread all over the world to deceive people. Do not persist to follow them thinking that you are being led by the true men of God. The last day is near. Be watchful!

Do not persevere in the things of the devil, but rather, persevere in the things of God in where there is a reward of eternal life in Heaven. Hallelujah! When you persevere in God, the devil surrenders and flees away from you. So, perseverance is also a weapon against the devil. Therefore, let us all have that weapon in us. Amen.

Finally, I say: put on the whole armor of God, and do not separate perseverance from supplication for all the saints. The two must go together, and also together with the other ones. Be fully equipped with the army-weapons of the Lord God. Hallelujah!

16. CLOSSING PRAYER

God, the Almighty Warrior, who dwells between the
Cherubim,

Great and awesome is Your name: Jehovah, the
Almighty.

I pray to thank You for delivering me from the hands
of the devil, and for equipping me with the whole
armor of Yours so that I may be able to stand against
the wiles of the devil.

May Your peace, teachings and deliverance dwell in
me forever and ever in Jesus Christ's name. Amen.

FOOTNOTES

The following are powerful books that have been mentioned and referred to in this book. I advise you should read them. They are so helpful indeed.

1. *HUMAN BEINGS CANNOT CHANGE WITHOUT PRESSURE* by Dr. E. H. Guti

This book encourages and strengthens us when we face challenges in our lives.

2. *DEMONS AND HOW TO DEAL WITH THEM* by Dag Heward-Mills

This one makes us understand and conquer our spiritual enemies. It gives us spiritual insight.

THE END

www.ingramcontent.com/pod-product-compliance
Lightning Source LLC
Chambersburg PA
CBHW060544030426
42337CB00021B/4420